T0161536

ORACLE FIGURES

ORACLE FIGURES

Eric Pankey

AUSABLE PRESS
2003

Cover art: Joseph Cornell, *Neptun au Lac* (Neptune at the Lake)
© The Joseph and Robert Cornell Memorial Foundation
Licensed by VAGA, New York, NY

Design and composition by Ausable Press.
The type is Adobe Jensen with Trajan titling.
Cover design by Rebecca Soderholm.

Published by
AUSABLE PRESS
1026 HURRICANE ROAD, KEENE NY 12942
www.ausablepress.com

Distributed by
SMALL PRESS DISTRIBUTION
800-869-7553
www.spdbooks.org

The Acknowledgements appear on page 76 and constitute
a continuation of the copyrights page.

Library of Congress Cataloging-in-Publication Data
Pankey, Eric, 1959—
Oracle figures : poems / by Eric Pankey. — 1st ed.
p. cm.
ISBN 1-931337-07-1 (alk. paper) — ISBN 1-931337-08-X (pbk. : alk. paper)
I. Title.

PS3566.A575073 2003
811'.54–dc21
2003001417

for my teachers
and in memory of George Tainter and Kathy Mitchell

ALSO BY ERIC PANKEY

Cenotaph (2000)

The Late Romances (1997)

Apocrypha (1991)

Heartwood (1988)

For the New Year (1984)

ORACLE FIGURES

I.

THE RECONSTRUCTION
OF THE FICTIVE SPACE

I open my eyes and a season passes:
A single moth wing shudders on the sill.
The gate cannot open into the overgrown grass.

But the way, lit by foxfire and firefly,
By the flint-flash of grit at the pearl's heart,
Is a past words cannot return to history,

To what the swallows inscribe on the air,
And here, on the outskirts of memory,
I look off again into that distance,

As if into a future, the lightning opening
Before my eyes like Scripture.
The equation at hand can be proven

By the spiral descent of the fishhawk,
By the curve of a tiger-lily's stalk.
Yet all I see is surface glare,

An afterlife of the afterimage.

ORACLE FIGURES

The soul is honey.
So say the fox tracks along the sandbank
Wind will smudge and rain efface.

I thought I could see the future,
But when I looked I saw the past:

Tied with a shoestring
And shelved on its side.
The binding's glue consumed by silverfish.

There is that moment
In the quarried dark of late winter
When a word begins to adhere to its object.

That moment, as all moments, is transitory.

In the garden of hours:
The thorn hour,
The husk hour,
The clove hour.

I waited for the wolf to devour the god,
To shake its head and scatter the bones,
To lap from the skull fermented honey.

Instead, fever,
Four humors fretted into a flame,
Ravened me.

My body a script
Read beneath the shadow lace of leaves,
Beneath the single grain of light the moon allotted.

The stars seen through the wire grid of the cage
Are what they are, and the cold, a dead language.
The depth of field and the field of vision, the dream
And its driftage, the dark's one garment dragged
Through the distant olive, are scribbled and hatched.
Doubt is part of the process of inquiry,
As is the single star downcast. As is the cricket.
As is the grass. As is the milk on a lynx's tongue.

Another constellation tilts into place.
The mesh of gears a hush I hear
As wind in the cypresses, wind in the ruins.

Each sentence I start to utter begins,
Once . . .
But all I find is a washed-out road.

Had there been a maple leaf
On the path, I would have picked it up
And saved it in this notebook

Between pages of words for *this* and *that*.
The moon cups the hillside monastery
In the curve of its scythe

Like a capital C in an illuminated manuscript.
I stand at the edge and let the pea gravel
Slip underfoot and over, all the way down to the city.

A scumble of lead white, coal soot,
And a brush's frayed, fugitive hairs:

New to full, full to new.
The window dark.
The window bellied with light.

At eye-level on the doorjamb,
The brittle jacket of the cicada.

Between a dream
And the residue of a dream,
The body a ghost sloughs.

The hazel rod of the *word*,
The augur of the *landscape*,

Written down in a calligraphy
So elaborate it was illegible:

Serifs, tendrils, knots, serpents,
An umbilical like a noose,
A thicket of thorns and bindweed

Where as a child I cut a tunnel
And in the cool maze of shadows
Slept until nightfall,

The spiders writing another story
In the empty spaces above.

The skiff, unmoored, leaves no mark
As it drifts out with the tide.
The coming storm drags its rain
Like a full net behind it.
If what we share is the waking,
Give me an ampule of dream.

If I squint my eyes I can see the floating world where all
   forms are born.
The white of the birch, the winter's only green, is whiter
   than hoarfrost.
I cast a hexagram of six broken lines. I cheated. Threw
   again.
*I threw the I Ching yesterday. It said there'd be thunder at the
   well.*
The word translated as "coaxed" means literally "as fingers
   change strings."
If I squint my eyes I can see the floating world where all
   forms are born.

Beneath a cirrus of chalk dust,
Beneath a penumbra of erasures:
Word traces, strata of equations,
Scansion marks, the day's lessons.

With a needle, I dig the splinter out:
The sliver, dislodged, minute.
The broken surface, the gist.

The body deciphers grief.
I wake at night to the click of its machinery.

Thus far, I have mapped the frayed fabric of a mirage,
Have let the past sift like bone meal into the soil.
What I had hoped to say was sweet, like lead on the tongue.

STRIKING THE COPPER BOWL TO
IMITATE THE SINGING DRAGON

All evening the dark bleeds through:
A shiver of loosestrife,
             Amethyst, then gray,

Rice-paper ink-washed,
An octopus spilled and tumbled
             From its nether-lair,

Then overexposed, white,
The drought haze backlit,
             Graphic with heat lightning.

Green-scaled, rare, awful,
The song of the dragon
             Is an anvil's bell,

A hammer-blow—a cold toll,
Rain-tempered,
             A song followed always by rain,

But nothing falls.
Except stars—leached salt,
        Bone meal through a sieve,

      Cold feral fire.
The wells failed.
        The reservoir empty.

EPITAPH

Beyond the traceries of the auroras,
The fires of tattered sea foam,
The ghost-terrain of submerged icebergs;
Beyond a cinder dome's black sands;
Beyond peninsula and archipelago,
Archipelago and far-flung islands,
You have made of exile a homeland,
Voyager, and of that chosen depth, a repose.

The eel shimmers and the dogfish darts,
A dance of crisscrosses and trespasses
Through distillate glints and nacreous silts,
And the sun, like fronds of royal palm
Wind-torn, tossed, lashes upon the wake,
But no lamplight mars or bleaches your realm,
A dark of sediment, spawn, slough, and lees,
Runoff, pitch-black, from the rivers of Psalms.

IMPROVISATION

The only bridge across Wind River is the wind.

This is not a poem, not a suture of words, not a voice without accompaniment.

The poem is what silence instigates: a sanctuary between "The Temptation" and "The Expulsion" furnished with footfalls and echoes, a way station between *rapture* and *rupture.*

Beneath the chandelier, a single wooden chair with a braided velvet cord draped over its arms. The poem is not the chair, but the reconfigured function of the chair: *to be seen.*

The wind rattles around in the heart like a janitor with hours still to go on his shift. And nothing left to clean.

Desire and its generation, its preservation, its fulfillment, its deterioration, its vanquishing, its loss, are the residue of the poem and not its source. When I say *the wind,* I mean *the poem.* When I say *the poem,* I mean *a variable in an equation.* When I say *I,* I mean *a voice without accompaniment.*

No one looking in the goat's eye mistakes it for a human eye. The devil's perhaps. Close enough to be the devil's eye. The little horns and the tuft of beard complete the mask. The poem is the expression of the actor behind the mask. The poem is the human eye that, from the theater's back row, seems goat-like in the devil mask.

Put a line through it. X it out: *The wind over the lip of the green bottle. The wind-frayed stamen.*

THE COORDINATES

Ten-thousand worlds in the eye of a deerfly
And I slap it against my thigh nonetheless.
So much for the multiplicities of awe.

For now, the horizon's tin edge separates
The figment of sky from the figment of hills.
The dull mileage between the Rappahannock

And Occoquan is but a blink of an eye.
When did the mere sublime fall out of favor?
When did the ineffable lose the sacred?

A spider bridges the gap between two oaks.
A black snake slips through a cowlick of tall grass.
I map the coordinates, take ragtag notes.

Sometimes I can put two and two together.
The wisteria shrugs beneath wind's weight,
Although I wasn't going the mention the wind,

That ghost-driven given, dry, pollen-thick,
Everywhere at once, then nowhere, where it lives.

THE FLAME

The flame is an object transformed by its displacement.
The flame is a qualm of zags and gnarls.

Between the match and the wick,
The rain turns to hail.

Between the match and the wick,
Pison, Tigris, Gihon, and Euphrates flood their banks.

My father refused to swim.
As a merchant marine, he went overboard

And was forced to cross an icy distance underwater,
A distance measured by a surface of burning oil.

The sky above black with smoke.
He would not even watch us swim.

Elusive, shuddered, shredded by a breath,
The flame unravels a configuration of shadow by which
     the world is known.

If all things are exchanged for fire,
Then there is no bridge over this burning ground.

The souls, as I reach out my hand, lean toward such solidity,
Then gutter like flames, retreat.

In the midst of telling my dream,
I remember only my waking.

The flame is wayward, an afterthought congealed,
Eros courted by Ambivalence, a canker,

The gaze of an icon, a thorn,
A shipwreck in a Romance.

How long has reason darkened my desire?
I hold my hand over the flame.

Between the flame and my hand, an equinox.
Between the flame and my hand, a grain of millet.

Between the flame and my hand,
The shallow night silted in with soot.

II.

THE OLD BRICKYARD QUARRY

The world begins with a gaze, impromptu,
The first light endlessly divisible,
Starless, submerged in vapor, unscored, loosed,

So that one does not think of proportion,
Abrupt edges, magnetic poles, remnants,
Or, for instance, the quality of mercy,

Or the maker. To dispense with narrative,
To let go of the ledger, the inventory,
The ten-thousand stains where blood redeemed,

Is to believe in the dream's irrational
Counter-history, the limestone scree,
The said and to-be-said held in solution,

The weight a body takes on, inch by inch,
As it's pulled from the quarry's clouded water,
A body bloated, radiant. Jade-tinged. Pearl.

A HEMISPHERE OF STARS

The figures, sticks, and dice
Shaken and cast,

(As if some milled grain and a single breath
Might animate the cosmos)

Shaken and cast
And read as *a bridge of ice,*

As the death of *the father,* the death of *the mother,*
A wagon-load of salt beneath a downpour,

As limestone like a bridge of ice
Undercut by a spring,

As the season of *the waste of mulberries,*
The season of *the shrug of drizzle,*

As an *axis* defined by the *interval of time*
One moves through in grieving;

An *axis* defined by the *mystical possibilities*
Of operations of chance;

As a graph *filled in* by a *hemisphere of stars.*
I was part of the conspiracy:

Each detail was made to equal the whole.
Shaken and cast and read

Until one reading is displaced by another,
Until the olive tree aflame is unburned,

Green in a grove of green,
Silver in a grove of silver.

SHADES BEFORE AN OFFERING

They stand before me as the stirred air
Outside a swarm, a ghost of salt
In suspension, shadow wrapped in shadow.

My habit of flame gives them shape:
A mass that tosses and settles, tosses
Like drafts in a wind, loose pages,

Scribbles amid the fog and ether,
Scribbles and scratches upon vellum.
No words can tempt them to step forward.

No barley or wine, blood or honey.
No opiate incense. No dram of sleep.
No words can tempt them to step forward

Again. They recognize my hands,
Folded in prayer, for what they are:
A rude shambles, the locus of slaughter.

MY MOTHER AMID THE SHADES

If you are my son, what proof do you offer?
I give you the annunciatory angel's lily.
I give you the rubric of Christ's hidden scripture.

If you are my son, these are not yours to offer.
I give you a wine bowl of ivy wood,
I give you four walls of wild pear, a roof of gold.

If you are my son, what proof do you offer?
I give you a field of windfall ripe with wasps.
I give you a single pear wrapped in tissue.

If *you are my son, these are not yours to offer.*
I give you the story of my father, your husband.
I give you all that was taken from him.

If you are my son, what proof do you offer?
None. The pyre, at last, translated all to ash.
At the border, they took everything, even his name.

POINT OF DEPARTURE

There along the continuum is the point
Where I almost disappear,
Not a vanishing point pierced through by each line,
But like the spot in the heat-thrummed shade of the
        thicket,
Tenuous, ephemeral, uncharted, yet open,
Into which the fox slips and is gone.

A wind lifts, shuffles, and repairs the tear.
One more drink and I'll call it quits.
One more drink and we'll see.

There, on either side of a bridge of magpies,
The evening and morning stars fixed within a window
        frame,
The torn paper of a wasps' nest,
The air warped above the mineral spirits, the house on
        fire.
Take it back, my brother would demand, his hands
At my throat. *Take it back.*

A spiral of swifts lifts from the chimney.
One more drink and I'll call it quits.
One more drink and we'll see.

THE CONSTELLATIONS OF AUTUMN

Who oversees this collect of caws, this clamor of crows, gathered by grace around a carcass?

Alas, our narrator is despondent [*from the Latin*, despondere, *meaning 'solemnly to undertake a promise'*] and having given his word, has nothing else to give.

It is not the rain that set the star-of-Bethlehem white above the valley. *Hath the rain a father?* It is not rain, but a hillside of white flowers.

Now is the hour for dousing the fire. The curfew. "Too much whiskey these days, late getting up/ I lie and watch the western hills, give up on unfinished poems."

Thomas Merton: "A postulant said this morning, 'How deep do they dig a grave? They have been at it all morning.'"

A sudden wind through the summerhouse. The constellations of autumn. The landscape a box of air. An empty reliquary. Error not erased but crossed out.

Aquinas believed poetry the lowliest of the sciences—it has little truth about it. I walk the Post Road and argue with Aquinas. Point out the thistle, the cornflowers.

Who would not curse the snake and its shadow? Who, in finding its papery skin snagged in brambles, does not begin to believe the Resurrection?

When the roll is called up yonder, when the roll is called up yonder, when the roll is called up yonder, when the roll is called up yonder, I'll be there.

Too much whiskey these days. Late in getting up. I lie and watch the western hills. The sun all haze. Read the poems of my teachers and go back to bed.

DUSK COLLOQUY WITH A GHOST

The dragonflies flick the tips of cattails,
Skim the scrim of the stagnant pond.

The moments shimmer by.
The day congeals as sluggish light.

As light through silt. As light through silk.

The water is deep enough, my friend argues, to drown a
       horse.
I say it looks shallow.

He tips back the bottle, takes a slug, passes the whiskey
       to me.

Soon, the broken blue tiles will fall.
Soon, the black lacquer will spill.

I cannot find my way, he says, by the atlas of the past.
I say deep enough to drown a man.

We'll need another bottle and the rest of the night,
He says, to get dead drunk.

I say deep enough to drown a man.

III.

NIGHT FISHING

My father stepped off the path.
Then my brother. I followed.

Even then I was a collector:
A quail feather, a bolus,
Chips of fool's gold,
Milkweed down, poplar seed.

I knew then as now
The tangible world,
The demands of nostalgia,
The cosmology's concentric circles.

They wait for me
Beside the cow pond
To find my way.

I collected elements for a divination kit:
A thimbleful of rusted filings.
A horseshoe magnet.

I knew then as now
How to read in sand
The movements of a snake.

They are there,
My father and brother.

How to fashion such a night?
Starlight snared in the amnion?

I finger each knot in the net bag
We will use as a creel
And find no flaw, no tear.

I navigate by the twin tips
Of their cigarettes,

The pulse of burn and dull,
Burn and dull:
The distance between us constant.

There must be a word that means
To knock repeatedly
On a door to gain entrance
And yet not gain entrance.

First my father disappears
Into the canebrake.
Then my brother.

SHELTER

[tinder for the wind]

The house is a house of straw, tinder for the wind,
A bed for a vagrant spark that calls itself *I.*

If knowledge is carnal, the sad arithmetic
Equals cold light. At times liquid. At times stone.

The hands and numerals, alive with radium,
Blur as I take off my glasses and go to sleep.

Out of the ether, out of the sarcophagus,
The night spreads threadbare on the lawns, on the houses.

Hold up a map detailing the lunar phases
And eclipses. With a burnt match, chart your way home.

[errata]

I counted the three species of fire,
The four rivers of Eden,
The five ghosts gathered at the blood,
   The devil's thousand names,
The winter wheat as yet unripe.

Slips and slurries of words
Blurred in memory.
Still, nothing equaled *one*,
   A past foreshortened,
A moment without void or form.

Just a cellar left
After the house fire.
   The ash within the ash
Nourished the flames.

From the levee, I watched
The rivers converge,
   The spirit-lamp of the moon
Annulled by its own reflection.

[in absentia]

I take as my shelter a mirage.
In these shadows, a legion of shadows shadow forth.
I pry up the subfloor's boards and find sand.

A rush of wind discloses the moon:
A sallow mandorla, a rust-pitted spearhead.
Where the fox stood, the undergrowth still shivers.

The furnace ticks, then gusts,
A crown of blue flame behind the grillwork.
Still, the house is cold.

A sudden drizzle casts its aspersion.
If I listen, I can hear the recluse spider
As it inches into exile.

[an eagle-headed genie watering the tree of life]

A thread of fragrance, as from garlands,
(The air hyacinthine, the air a fissure of rain)

As from a thousand-petaled lotus,
Lifts as I turn the leaf of a manuscript,

Until what was sky-clad,
What was over-scored with ashen earthshine—

This aqueous sphere—dims,
And I am left in the dark, vexed,

A minor participant in a great event,
A reader in the dark where the planets pass.

[black bile]

I avoid the inward gaze,
Where I know the words wait—opaque, leaden—
Like the perfumes and clutter on a vanity.

I keep time by the swing of a censer,
By the sullen inertia of the mineral kingdom.
For so long, I looked and stared,

Believing the *out-there* would reveal a glimpse
That might dislodge this aphasia.
A quandary of crows above the wood's one path

Caws a cartography of elsewhere,
An ægis under which I walk.

[reading the ancients]

I say melancholy is sweet milk when I know it's alum.

The story is always the same: one thing leads to another.

The iris unsheathes behind a screen of rain. A fern stays
    furled.

The sparrow hath its home and the swallow its nest. Fair
    enough.

How soon the light changes—glare to wan, steeped to
    seared to tarnished.

Though no one plays, the piano turner still comes once a
    year.

I like to hear the keys tested, the notes bent back into
    shape.

It's hard not to envy the practicality of his skill.

For me, for years, depression has been my shelter.

It looks like I'm moving, Bob Dylan sings, *but I'm standing still.*

ECLIPSE OF THE SUN OBSERVED THROUGH A PINHOLE

The name of the thing escapes me:
My mind these days a depth of erasures,

Hatch-marks, scrawled figures, signs smeared to dust,
The final note of the octave between dusk

And dawn unsounded, yet there like a thorn
To snag, to un-thread a dream, to unravel

Like a sentence that one knows from the start
Should be reeled back in before it tangles,

Before one conjunction or another—
Therefore, but, and, however—sets the stranded

Argument into motion, the maze of,
The proliferation of the *this* and the *this*,

The ruse of examples: *The cottonwoods
In the hollow*, or *the magpie's treasury*,

Or *Mars amid the stark congregation of stars,*
Before one prefers the enumeration of difference,

Before one prefers the digression,
The breath one takes to speak then does not.

THE LESSON OF SNAKES

The seedpods of the catalpa drooped and curled,
And the red ant traced the ravine's limestone ridge,
Followed the length of roots and fossils down
To the water's edge, to a torn, wind-shuddered,
Ragged wing, matted and speckled with dry blood.
The farmer's far field—harrowed, unsown, fallow—
Gave up whirlwinds of dust until the rain fell,
Until mosquitoes, bred in those furrows, thronged,
Their whine a counterpoint to the transformers,
To the gusts swaying the high tension wires.
The garter and ringneck taught me to crawl
From the wood's green-dark and mercurial womb,
The water moccasin to drowse in the shade
Of branch and cold depths, undertow and thorn hedge.
I lay face-down in the dust and waited
For the eclipsed sun, quick-cooled like molten lead,
Like a drop of pine sap, an abacus bead—
Sum, multiple, quotient, remainder of all—
To burn. To burn at last. To enliven me.

A DEAD CROW ON GOOD FRIDAY

The wing's torn black iridescence, flint-edged,
Once a dynasty of shimmers and glosses,
Shines, if it shines at all, as rain-slick char in the curfew
    light, the truant light, light that strays.

One could renounce, at this point, the gaze—*look away!*—
But no, the lens has been ground
At great expense and, held at the right distance, magnifies
    and clarifies the tremors and aftershocks,

The tabulation of tenebrous light and shadow,
Shadow and light that stay nothing, that hold
No moment in their moment, the moment verging, mutable,
    unfixed, at once *here* and *hereafter*.

One would expect a gash, as sudden and lush
As the redbud along the spring-fed creek;
One would expect splayed viscera, split ribs, the ribs picked
    clean of maggots by thrush and starlings,

Yet in the crow's cold eye, the malformed sky opens a com-
    pendium of clouds.
In its cold eye, where later ants will forage,
A shadowed valley, one's own inverted reflection, distorted,
    almost familiar.

FOR THIS WORLD

I descended through a sinkhole—The Devil's Icebox—
And as I entered the depth of the cave, the daylight—

Stark, straight, and astringent, a pollen-dusted column—
Seemed a mythic ladder between earth and below,

A fissure to the chill damp of flowstones and cave springs.
All summer I returned. Belly-down or hunched or stalled,

Back-tracking, taking a different fork, my eyes at home
In the grainy distances my flashlight cut and opened.

A darkness that could repair itself in an instant.
Among the elect, I was innocent of my fate.

Among the damned, I was innocent of my fortune.
If only I could delve deeper, I thought, I might find

Magma, the very threshold of hell, its door ajar.
But nothing banked the cold, the clean cold, the limestone
        air.

When I returned to the surface, the blunt light dazzled
On the quick creek, the oak- and maple-strewn ridge,

The moss, the lichen constellations on the sinkhole's edge.
I would look back down into the darkness until my eyes

Adjusted, until my eyes were ready for this world.

HISTORY

A hundred flint arrowheads, chipped, rain-washed, scat-
    tered through a meadow of ragweed and clover,
The flesh they ripped, the rib nicked, the shields of horse-
    hide torn, all lost to the elements;
An ice-pierced daybreak through a mica screen and the first
    lute arrives in China from Persia;

The uses of ambergris are perfected; the lamb's blood dries
    above the doorway; a glacier calves an iceberg;
From the rock where a father offered up his son as sacrifice,
    the Prophet ascends into paradise;
The summer you step on a rusted nail, the willows green
    and bend to the river; the river floods;

Before nightfall, a body is bargained for, secreted away in a
    borrowed grave fashioned from a cave;
Again, walls and towers topple. And no language but grief
    is left in common. And grief no language at all.
There is no history, only fits and starts, laughter at the
    table, lovers asleep, slaughter, the forgetfulness,

And yet for three nights straight, nothing but starlight—
    Byzantine, quicksilver, an emanation of a past—
And tonight you have renamed the constellations after
    the mudras: *The Gesture Beyond Mercy,*
The Gesture for Warding Off Evil, The Gesture of Fearlessness,
    The Gift-Bestowing Gesture of Compassion.

IV.

VALEDICTION

The Thames is a Mississippian umber beneath Blackfriars
    Bridge,
The sky, an enclave of gray clouds.

Only the past is a deep-blue,
A glass prepared from silica and potash,
Oxide of cobalt pulverized as pigment.

The Marquis de Sade requested acorns be scattered over
    his grave
So that an oak grove would obliterate its location.

If we let the dead bury the dead,
Perhaps all requests would be honored.
But the living bury the dead.

Small wonder the compass needle points its one way,
Shimmering like a divining rod's trance.
It was only today, I admit, that I noticed the anagram *Eros*
    in the rose.

MATERIA PRIMA

[small corpus]

There where the thread breaks,
There where the prayers are blown out
With the votives,
                              a zodiac of live coals,
A loose cursive script
Of pine soot ink and clear water
Defining the fog and mountains.

The broken spine of a book
Hinges autumn to winter.

When she touches his eyelids
He shuts them.

The book, a book of songs,
Falls open to:
                              the lily among the thorns.
To: *a bundle of myrrh.*

When she touches his eyelids,
When she touches her tongue to his nipple,

He sees a sky as blue as the god's body.

[dance glyphs]

The riddle begins: *the deer enters the winter arbor.*
The riddle begins: *the second cutting, the aftermath.*

Her right hand opened in the gesture of forgiveness.
Her left in the gesture of compassion.

The moon—a copper souvenir oxidized to green,
A mottled chip of fallen plaster, mineral-stained—
Is eclipsed by the lamp the sleeping lovers left on.

The riddle begins: *a harvest of frosts.*
The riddle begins: *the orb of air in the spirit level.*

Above them, the analects of stars.

In his dream, the Northern Lights curve away
Like a curl of wood from a lathe.

In her dream, he steps into a skiff
Built to ferry ghosts.

The riddle begins: *the far bank of the river—*

[mask with red]

From the seven windows, she could see the seven moun-
    tains that house the seven gods.
From the seven windows, he watched the smoke, hun-
    kered on the river, not rise.

The red: tea of rose petals. Rust. Staghorn of the sumac.
    A pin-prick of blood.
The mask: *kanji* on lambskin. The face of a wind. Con-
    sort to the barn owl.

From the seven windows, he watched birds steal straw
    from the lawn, leaving seed exposed.
From the seven windows, she could see the seven moun-
    tains that house the seven gods.

When she wore the mask, he could feel her touch every
    where at once.
When he wore the mask, he stumbled, as in a game of
    blindman's bluff.

[celadon]

How long before the dew basin overflowed,
Before the gauze sleeve embroidered
    With a knot of dragons
Became wind across a stony draw?

He says: *My heart is a cave of spirits.*
He says: *My heart is a splintered sound-box.*
She says: *I know.*
She says: *I know.*

When the crow lifts, a little snow
Shivers down from the branches.

She says: *I love that color.*
Meaning: the dusk air between the apple and pear orchards.
Meaning: the backlit wasps' nest.
Meaning: the glazed shard among the coral and carnelian.

How long before the moon dissolved
Like sugar under the tongue?
    Before the green ice broke up?
Before the creek, swollen with runoff,

Eddied around an oar of orchid wood?

[skull with thought]

At dusk, the channel markers seem unmoored,
Adrift in the drift of the oncoming night.

Always a little song to spin from the pain:
Always a little song to spin from the pain . . .

Her window is unlit. His dream is an abandoned draft,
A watermark below the surface of the seen.

Nothing seems worthy to hang upon the nail,
So it remains the white wall's one ornament.

[materia prima]

She was to him as distance is to a traveler.
He was to her the three compass points not followed.
    That is where the story ends,
And without a mention of *northwest* or *southeast*
Or *how far* or *the one-thousand labors in between.*

The telling begins: *In that time . . .*
And each teller, who might tell the story, goes from there—
    The lead, or bronze, or iron, white hot,
Is poured over the lip of such an overture,
And what we thought was the story,

What took the shape of the story,
Vanishes like lost wax.

[corpus]

Her husband, of course, imagined the god's body
Intertwined with hers,

Merged—a white mineral flame,
Radiant, involuted, churning.

The rest of the story, she insisted,
Was of no account.

He held her through the night,
Through a dream's argument,

Through an August rain
That did not cool the summerhouse.

Her body. My body, he added.
Always two. Joined by *and.* Held apart by *or.*

Later she scattered thistle seed
To attract the mourning doves,

And two came, skittish at first.
She scattered more and they stayed all day.

PIAZZA S. SPIRITO NO. 9

I will always love this light: the brayed clarity of gypsum,
    the cool kiln-glow of amber,
No longer liquid, not yet stone.

And the green shutter creaked by a breeze. And, across
    the courtyard, the laundry pulleyed in,
Echoing a song of rhymes: *toll, coal, squall, straw, strewn* . . .

And the table set with a vase of lavender, the table level on
    the shim of a closed matchbook.
And the sleep easy afterward, the heavy sleep of the body
    unencumbered by dream or memory,

My body cradled in the luminous idleness of your own.

VENETIAN AFTERTHOUGHT

If a lit chandelier is lowered
Slowly by rope then a lit chandelier
Rises slowly from the canal's murk,

From mildew's blues and silvers,
From the foretold and forestalled depths.

If a star falls at the sky's edge—
Ash of a flicked cigarette,
A glyph of smoke that picks a lock—

Then the Gates of the Resurrection open
Onto a maze, a riddle of interstices.

If and *then*. *If* and *then*.
One always leading in this dance.
The other making it look inevitable.

Yet there, on the zinc door of dusk,
Not a peephole, but Venus.

A rope dangles, half-submerged,
From the landing like an untrimmed wick in oil.

And the gates, bitten by salt air and rust, lie unhinged.

TABLEAU

As if to repair the apparent,
Or anneal with the flame of a gaze,
I look out, behold the pied and patched,
A redwing blackbird like a shuttle
Slipped between threads of shadow and light,
The leaves shuffled, the leaves unshuffled,
The barbican of the marsh cedar,
The talcum smear of the late day-moon.
As if by noting here the pieces,
The peculiar, the particulars,
The immanent might disclose itself.

Oyster River. Low tide. Seventeen years
I've crossed the bridge into town and back.
I glance over the river's ghost flux,
The scriptorium of its surface,
Where the sky is copied and copied,
Recomposed as a writ of transport,
The wind-smoothed wakes as gospel and acts.
One can hope to pin down a meaning:
August dusk as an intersection
Of one rare imaginary line
And another, a place mapped and fixed.

As if in one landscape, I am one
Person, in another another,
I slide through the chameleon changes:
At night, a fall of Pompeian ash
On the prairie flats of a snowfield;
At night, the river at Deep River.
The star-glut wrangled, its edges fenced
With chicken wire and flat furred slats.
At the apex of Purgatory,
The selves-I-am-not are not yet pure.
The self-I-am not yet self. Nor pure.

Smoke above the wet wood warps and sags,
Snags in the weed-spikes, in winter's
Tarnished tines. At the dry-leaf beech fringe,
A cold ministry of crows (angels
In a life without angels) extolls
A finale without conclusion.
The runnels, quick with ice-melt, crisscross.
Seconds pass in silence like an owl.
I am waiting for the flame to turn
Inside out, to step from its robes,
To extinguish the flint-dusk's white noise.

I hold my breath but hold back nothing:
The past a thousand places behind
The decimal point, a thousand and one
Stories retold while I hold my breath.
Two weeks since the vernal equinox.
The moon, moon-lit itself, is a trapdoor.
Now, when I should look down, I look out
To the white dogwood afloat on air.
I hold my breath and hold nothing back.
Tonight *is*, yet is at a remove.
At such a remove, a night begins.

FINAL THOUGHT

What I have argued thus far is but a treatise
On the owl and the moon, as if the given
Were world enough, as if one thousand and one

Views of the moon—each phase marked, inscrutable—
Illumined the hairline crack in the plaster,
The door to the river, midwinter's passage,

A field of view inverted through a pinhole.
The terrestrial and celestial globes
Are not translations of figured worlds,

But worlds figured, where the owl flushed from the oak
Circles above a lost plan of paradise,
The tumbled onyx wall, the enclosure's gate.

All is shaped by the moon's static glare and verge,
Its cold charge, by talon, span, plummet, and swerve.
Awake I read the script of a reverie,

Parse and dissect a reed shaken by the wind,
And asleep the *Ars Magna Lucis et Umbrae*,
The monocle of the shallow fire pond,

The surface lux, lumen, color, and splendor,
Silvers and salts from which the image appears.
Between waking and sleeping, I smudge the chalk

Of the plumb line, behold a heaven so vast
No word can stain it. An object's flawless fact
As it is desired is, in fact, its flaw,

The object's flaw the fact of its attraction:
The mimicry of lack and want, want and lack,
The melancholy of *there is . . .* and *there is . . .*

The owl and moon are points of departure.
Pythagoras read the moon in a mirror,
Divined the future. The owl is my augur:

Talon, span, plummet, and swerve, silence subsumed
Into silence, a final thought that tightens
Like a slipknot around nothing and undoes itself.

LEAVE-TAKING ABOVE
THE MISSOURI

The way out is up, over, through the thistle gate, the
    abrupt bluffs, ten thousand trees,
Harder than the journey in: a spatterdash of leaf-light,
    switchbacks, cold's empty quiver.

We follow the etiquette of leave-taking: each turning
    once to wave,
Then not turning until the other is beyond sight. By
    then we are tired.

We share one heart and in it a spent quarry fills with
    rainwater.
I am re-begot of absence, darkness, death, you quoted Donne,
    Things which are not.

Late nights we talked like that. The world was new: the
    raw starlight. The river.
The shape of the shifting sandbar. The third glass of
    wine, it seemed, a finer vintage than the first.

ACKNOWLEDGEMENTS

I am deeply grateful to the editors of the following journals in which these poems, often in different versions, first appeared and first found readers:

American Poetry Review: The Constellations of Autumn

Antioch Review: Materia Prima [*dance glyphs*]

Bellingham Review: Shelter [*errata*]

Cimarron Review: The Flame, Materia Prima [*celadon*]

Denver Quarterly: A Hemisphere of Stars

Field: The Coordinates

Frantic Egg: Night Fishing

The Gettysburg Review: Improvisation

Image: A Journal of Arts and Religion: History

The Kenyon Review: Materia Prima [*small corpus*], Striking the Copper Bowl to Imitate the Singing Dragon, The Lesson of Snakes, Epitaph, Shelter [*in absentia*], Venetian Afterthought

Meridian: For This World, Oracle Figures, Point of Departure

Natural Bridge: Shades Before an Offering, My Mother Amid the Shades

The New England Review: The Reconstruction of the Fictive Space

The New Republic: Materia Prima [*materia prima*]

River Styx: Dusk Colloquy With a Ghost

Sou'wester: Shelter [*black bile*], Shelter [*tinder for the wind*], Eclipse of the Sun Observed through a Pinhole

Spirituality and Health: Dead Crow on Good Friday

Verse: Materia Prima [*mask with red*], Materia Prima [*skull with thought*], Piazza S. Spirito No. 9

Virginia Quarterly Review: Shelter [*an eagle-headed genie watering the tree of life*], Final Thoughts

The Yale Review: The Old Brickyard Quarry

These poems are dedicated as follows: "Celadon" and "Piazza S. Spirito No. 9" to Jennifer Atkinson, "The Constellations of Autumn" to Michael Friedman, "For This World" to Allison Funk, "Epitaph" to Barbara Jordan, "Valediction" to Steve Schreiner, "Improvisation" to Peter Streckfus, "Shelter" to Eileen Sypher, "Striking the Copper Bowl to Imitate the Singing Dragon" to Charles Wright. I would like to thank Anita LaGamma for the gift of the book *Art and Oracle: African Art and Rituals of Divination* by Alisa LaGamma at the time when I was revising the title sequence. This book was completed with a generous fellowship from The John Simon Guggenheim Memorial Foundation and with the support and friendship of my colleagues at George Mason University. As always, with love and thanks to Jennifer and Clare for their company and kindness.